While every precaution has been taken in the preparation of this book, the publisher assumes no responsibility for errors or omissions, or for damages resulting from the use of the information contained herein.

MASTERING ANGULAR 16: A CONCISE OVERVIEW

First edition. July 3, 2023.

Copyright © 2023 Pedro Martins.

ISBN: 979-8223912248

Written by Pedro Martins.

Table of Contents

BY PEDRO MARTINS

MASTERING ANGULAR 16: A CONCISE OVERVIEW

Pedro Martins

FROM THE CREATOR OF "CANTINHODE.NET"

Mastering Angular 16: A Concise Overview

Master of Angular 16 Series

Pedro Martins

4th July 4, 2023

Book Introduction

"Mastering Angular 16: A Concise Overview" is an in-depth guide designed to navigate the reader through the landscape of modern web development using the latest features and improvements brought by Angular 16. This book aims to provide a comprehensive understanding of the concepts, techniques, and patterns necessary to harness the power of Angular 16, one of the most popular open-source web application development frameworks.

Angular 16, an evolution of its previous versions, comes with a diamond mine of features that significantly enhance the control of state changes, provide faster page loading, and drastically reduce construction time in various scenarios. This book will delve into these features and provide the reader with a practical understanding of how to use them effectively.

The first part of the book introduces Angular 16 and its core concepts, followed by a thorough exploration of its latest features such as **Angular Signals, Enhanced Hydration, esbuild** support, and many more. The middle chapters focus on more advanced topics, including the transition to **Ivy** with the removal of **Ngcc**, the creation and use of standalone components, and the optimization of **JavaScript bundles**.

In the latter part of the book, we delve into more complex aspects of Angular 16, such as **routing** with **component inputs, migrating** and **scaffolding standalone components, enforcing component directives** with required inputs, and understanding the use of **takeUntilDestroyed** and **DestroyRef**. We also explore the support for **Tailwind CSS**, a highly popular utility-first CSS framework that can be used to style your Angular applications.

The final chapters of the book are dedicated to discussing advanced Angular 16 **techniques, best practices, and the construction of a real-world project using the skills** and **knowledge acquired** throughout the book.

Whether you are a novice developer wanting to learn Angular or a seasoned professional aiming to update your knowledge to the latest version, "Mastering Angular 16: A Concise Overview" offers you a complete, easy-to-understand, and hands-on approach to mastering Angular 16."

Chapter 0: Setup of Angular 16

AFTER COMPLETING THE mentioned steps, you will have a basic setup for an Angular 16 project. You can begin developing your application by modifying the files in the project directory, including components, templates, and styles. Keep in mind that the provided steps are general guidelines, so it's advisable to refer to the official Angular documentation and other resources for more comprehensive information and additional setup choices.

Chapter 1: Introduction to Angular 16

THIS CHAPTER PROVIDES an overview of Angular 16 and its evolution from previous versions. It introduces the core concepts of Angular and the enhancements brought by the latest version.

Chapter 2: State Control with Angular 16 Signals

CHAPTER 2 DELVES INTO the newest feature of *Angular 16: Signals*. This feature enhances the control of state changes in applications. Readers will learn how to adjust signals by invoking them with a new value through the "*set()*" method and retrieve values using

the "*get()*" method. Practical examples and code snippets will illustrate how signals work and how to effectively use them in Angular applications.

Chapter 3: Enhanced Hydration: Reusing DOM Nodes

IN THIS CHAPTER, WE explore the concept of *'hydration'* in Angular 16. Unlike previous versions where Angular would discard pre-existing DOM nodes, Angular 16 allows developers to reuse these nodes, contributing to faster page loading. We'll discuss the scenarios in which this feature proves beneficial and how to implement it in your applications.

Chapter 4: Speeding Up Your Builds with esbuild

THIS CHAPTER INTRODUCES the *esbuild* developer preview in *Angular CLI* version 16. We'll cover how *esbuild* can drastically reduce the construction time in various scenarios. We'll also look at the integration with *Vite*, which allows the *CLI* to utilize Vite as its development server. This chapter includes practical examples of setting up a new build using *esbuild*.

Chapter 5: Transitioning to Ivy: The Removal of Ngcc

CHAPTER 5 IS DEDICATED to one of the significant changes in Angular 16: the removal of the *Angular Compatibility Compiler* (*ngcc*). The chapter discusses the transition from the View Engine to

Ivy, explaining what this means for developers and how it affects the Angular bundle size. We also explain the implications for using Angular View Engine modules in the new version.

Chapter 6: Standalone Components: The Power of Independence

CHAPTER 6 IS DEDICATED to introducing standalone components, a revolutionary feature that transforms the development and organization of applications. With standalone components, developers can modularize their code, creating self-contained entities that can seamlessly integrate into any Angular project. These components are independent and self-aware, improving code reusability, maintainability, and scalability.

Chapter 7: Optimizing JavaScript Bundles with Angular CLI

CHAPTER 7 IS DEDICATED to showing you the best practices for configuring bundling in Angular 16 to optimize your application's JavaScript bundle size and improve performance. Use the Angular CLI and the angular.json file to configure bundling options. Implement code splitting to load code on-demand and reduce the initial bundle size. Leverage optimization techniques like tree shaking and externalizing dependencies and more.

Chapter 8: Simplifying Routing with Component Inputs

CHAPTER 8 IS DEDICATED to simplifying routing in Angular 16 by passing router data as component inputs. Update to Angular 16 and enable the "bindToComponentInputs" option in the routing configuration. Declare @Input properties in components to receive route data and access it directly. By binding route data to component inputs, you enhance data utilization and improve the developer experience in Angular 16, eliminating the need for manual subscription and retrieval of route parameters.

Chapter 9: Migrating and Scaffolding Standalone Components

CHAPTER 6 IS DEDICATED to migrating to standalone components in Angular 16, which eliminates ngModules and allows components to declare their own dependencies. To migrate components, follow the Angular documentation, converting them to standalone components and removing unnecessary NgModule classes.

Chapter 10: Required Inputs: Enforcing Component Directives

COMPONENT DIRECTIVES, which specify component instantiation, processing, and usage at runtime, are introduced in Chapter 6.

Chapter 11. Understanding takeUntilDestroyed and DestroyRef

THE TAKEUNTILDESTROYED operator and the DestroyRef class, which are crucial for managing subscriptions and preventing memory leaks in components, will be explained and put to use in this chapter 11.

Chapter 12: Styling Your Angular Applications with Tailwind CSS

STYLING YOUR ANGULAR Applications with Tailwind CSS: We will have an introduction in this chapter.

Chapter 13: Advanced Angular 16 Techniques

ADVANCED ANGULAR 16 Techniques are introduced in this chapter.

Chapter 14: Best Practices for Angular 16 Development

SOME BEST PRACTICES for Angular 16 Development are covered in this chapter.

Chapter 15: Building a Real-World Project with Angular 16

IN THIS CHAPTER, WE will create a real-world application and apply all the new features present in Angular 16.

Chapter 0: Setup of Angular 16

To set up Angular 16, you can follow these general steps:

1. Install Node.js

ANGULAR REQUIRES NODE.js to run and manage dependencies. Download and install the latest version of Node.js from the official website (https://nodejs.org).

2. Install Angular CLI

ANGULAR CLI IS A COMMAND-line interface that simplifies Angular development tasks. Open a terminal or command prompt and run the following command to install Angular CLI globally:

npm install -g @angular/cli

3. Create a New Angular Project

USE ANGULAR CLI TO generate a new Angular project. Open a terminal or command prompt, navigate to the desired directory, and run the following command:

ng new my-app

This will create a new Angular project named "my-app" in a folder of the same name. Angular CLI will set up the project structure and install the necessary dependencies.

4. Navigate to the Project

CHANGE TO THE PROJECT'S directory by running the following command:

cd my-app

5. Serve the Application

START A DEVELOPMENT server and serve the Angular application by running the following command:

ng serve

This will compile the application and launch a development server. By default, the application will be accessible at `*http://localhost:4200*`.

These steps provide a basic setup for an Angular 16 project. You can now start developing your application by editing the files in the project directory, including the components, templates, and styles.

Please note that the provided steps are general guidelines, and it's always a good idea to consult the official Angular documentation and other resources for more detailed information and additional setup options.

Chapter 1: Introduction to Angular 16

A ngular 16, released on May 3, 2023, is a major version of the popular web application framework developed by Google, and it brings a myriad of enhancements and new features to improve development experience and application performance.

Key Features and Improvements

Improved Reactivity Model

ANGULAR 16 INTRODUCES a new reactivity model, which enhances performance and simplifies mental models for reactivity. It provides developers with the flexibility to choose reactivity management methods and enhances debugging capabilities.

Esbuild-based Build System

ANGULAR 16 INTRODUCES an esbuild-based build system, which has demonstrated a significant 72% improvement in cold production builds during its developer preview stage.

Binding Router Information to Component Inputs

DEVELOPERS CAN NOW directly bind router data, resolved router data, params, and queryParams to component inputs. This feature reduces reliance on ActivatedRoute and eliminates the need for boilerplate code, thereby making development easier and increasing code readability.

TakeUntilDestroyed and DestroyRef

ANGULAR 16 INTRODUCES `destroyRef` and `takeUntilDestroyed`, two RxJS operators that serve as replacements for the `ngOnDestroy` lifecycle hook. These operators facilitate a more functional coding style and handle cleanup of signal effects internally, eliminating the need for manual cleanup.

Jest Testing Framework

THE JEST TESTING FRAMEWORK, a popular testing tool in JavaScript ecosystems, is now experimentally supported in Angular 16, offering developers an alternative testing option.

Support for TypeScript 5.0

ANGULAR 16 INCLUDES support for TypeScript 5.0, which is particularly beneficial for ECMAScript decorators that extend JavaScript classes.

Other Improvements

ADDITIONAL ENHANCEMENTS in Angular 16 include the ability to convert signals to observables using the `rxjs-interop` module, the ability to specify a nonce attribute for component styles, and the use of self-closing tags in Angular templates.

Benefits for Developers and Businesses

ANGULAR 16 BENEFITS both developers and businesses alike. Developers can enjoy a more efficient and seamless development experience, with features like simplified mental models for reactivity, and the flexibility to choose reactivity management methods.

MASTERING ANGULAR 16: A CONCISE OVERVIEW

For businesses, Angular 16 brings improvements to Web Core Vitals, better SEO, and accessibility through server-side rendering. The support for TypeScript 5.0 and the ability to bind route parameters to component inputs further enhance productivity and code quality.

In summary, Angular 16 is a stable, robust, and feature-rich release that continues the tradition of Angular's commitment to improving web development experience and application performance.

Chapter 2: State Control with Angular 16 Signals

Definition of Angular 16 Signals

Angular 16 introduces a new feature called **Signals** for reactive state management. The **Signals** are functions that can be updated with new values and depend on other signals, creating a reactive value graph. They offer advantages over traditional change detection in Angular and are particularly inspired by **Solid.js**.

The Signals can be used to create services that store state. These services allow easy modification and access to properties. The class **SignalsSimpleStoreService** is used to define the state and is initialized with an empty object. The set and **setState** methods are used to update the state.

Signals are wrappers around values that notify consumers of changes. They can be writable or read-only. For instance, they can be used in TypeScript to update the total price in an e-commerce application's shopping cart. **Signals** can also be used to create effects that are executed when the value of a signal changes. In a provided example, effects are created for signals "foo" and "bar". When the "changeFoo" function is called, only the effects referencing the **"foo"** signal are executed. The effect referencing the "bar" signal is not executed because it doesn't reference **"foo"**.

Signals simplify the process of handling events and communication between components by providing observables that emit values, allowing components to subscribe and react accordingly. This enhances code cleanliness and maintainability, offering a fresh approach to event handling in Angular development.

Signals serve as reactive building blocks that enable precise change detection. They allow components to trigger change detection when the signal value changes. Examples demonstrate the usage of signals for binding properties in Angular components.

To use **Signals**, you can import the Signal class from **@angular/core** and create a new signal using the constructor. You can subscribe to signals using the **subscribe**() method and create computed values using the | async pipe.

Example of code on Angular 16 Signals

THIS IS A SIMPLE EXAMPLE of using Angular 16 **Signals** to manage state in an application. Note that this is a simple example and real-world applications may require a more complex setup based on our requirements.

Before we start, make sure to have Angular 16 installed in your development environment. If not, update your Angular version by running the following command:

bash

ng update @angular/cli@16 @angular/core@16

Let's create a simple service that uses **Signals** to manage state. We'll create a shopping cart service that holds the list of items in the cart.

```typescript
import { Signal } from '@angular/core';
export class ShoppingCartService {
private items: Signal<string[]> = new Signal([]);
getItems() {
return this.items;
}
addItem(item: string) {
this.items.value = [...this.items.value, item];
}
removeItem(item: string) {
this.items.value = this.items.value.filter(i => i !== item);
}
}
```

In the above code, we first import the *Signal* from *@angular/core*. We then create a *Signal* for the *items* in the cart. When an item is added or removed, we update the *items* signal.

Now let's create a component that uses this service.

```typescript
import { Component } from '@angular/core';
import { ShoppingCartService } from './shopping-cart.service';
@Component({
selector: 'app-shopping-cart',
template: `
<div *ngFor="let item of cartItems | async">
{{ item }}
<button (click)="removeItem(item)">Remove</button>
</div>
<input [(ngModel)]="newItem" placeholder="New Item" />
<button (click)="addItem()">Add to cart</button>
`,
})
export class ShoppingCartComponent {
cartItems = this.shoppingCartService.getItems();
newItem = '';
constructor(private shoppingCartService: ShoppingCartService) {}
addItem() {
if (this.newItem) {
this.shoppingCartService.addItem(this.newItem);
this.newItem = '';
}
}
removeItem(item: string) {
this.shoppingCartService.removeItem(item);
}
}
```

In the component, we use the **ShoppingCartService** to manage the cart items. We use the *async* pipe to subscribe to the *items* signal. When the *items* signal changes, the component will automatically update.

Remember, the above is a very simple example. Depending on your application's requirements, you might need more complex state management solutions. Always consider your application's specific needs when deciding on a state management strategy.

16

Chapter 3: Enhanced Hydration: Reusing DOM Nodes

Definition of Enhanced Hydration: Reusing DOM Nodes

The term "hydration" in the context of a web application refers to the process of taking server-rendered HTML and making it interactive by attaching event listeners to the DOM nodes. Traditionally, Angular would re-render the entire DOM tree in the client. However, Angular 16 introduced a new feature called non-destructive hydration which improves the hydration process.

In traditional hydration, the server sends a static HTML file to the client, and the client-side JavaScript then goes through the DOM tree and replaces the static content with dynamic content. This can be an expensive operation, especially for large web pages, because it involves recreating the entire DOM tree.

With non-destructive hydration, Angular 16 takes a more efficient approach. Instead of re-rendering the entire DOM tree, Angular now looks up the existing DOM nodes and attaches event listeners to them. This eliminates the need for re-rendering from scratch, which can lead to significant performance improvements, particularly for server-side rendered applications. This means that the DOM nodes that were created during server-side rendering are being reused on the client side, hence the term "reusing DOM nodes".

This is a big leap forward for Angular in terms of optimizing performance and developer experience. This feature makes Angular more competitive with other frameworks that have already implemented similar techniques. It's also worth mentioning that this improved hydration process aids in enhancing Web Core Vitals, which can lead to better SEO and accessibility for applications built with Angular 16.

Example of code on Angular 16 Enhanced Hydration

HERE IS AN EXAMPLE of how to enable this feature in your Angular application:

Firstly, you need to import the ***provideClientHydration*** function in your ***app.module.ts***:

```typescript
import { provideClientHydration } from '@angular/core';
```

```
```

Then add it to the providers array:

```typescript
@NgModule({
//...
providers: [provideClientHydration()],
//...
})
export class AppModule { }
```

ONCE YOU'VE ADDED THE `provideClientHydration` function to the providers, you can call the `hydrate()` method on the `ApplicationRef` to hydrate the application:

```typescript
import { ApplicationRef } from '@angular/core';
constructor(appRef: ApplicationRef) {
appRef.hydrate();
}
```

Calling the **hydrate()** method allows Angular to manage the application state and respond to user inputs. This approach improves application performance by minimizing the work required for application loading and can potentially lower memory usage.

Please note that you should always test new features in a non-production environment first to ensure that they work as expected and do not introduce any unintended side effects.

Angular 16 Reusing DOM Nodes

IN ANGULAR, THERE ARE several techniques for manipulating the Document Object Model (DOM). These include using template reference variables, *ElementRef*, *@ViewChild/@ViewChildren*, and the *AfterViewInit* lifecycle hook. Angular *Universal*, on the other hand, is a tool that allows server-side rendering of Angular applications. One of the challenges with *Angular Universal* is that it renders the HTML on the server but does not reuse the DOM nodes in the client.

Angular 16 introduces new features such as *Signals*, *DestroyRef*, *takeUntilDestroyed*, and the ability to bind router information to component inputs. Although none of these features directly addresses the re-hydration of DOM nodes as per our subject, they provide new mechanisms for managing component state and lifecycle, which could indirectly aid in the efficient reuse of DOM nodes.

For instance, *takeUntilDestroyed* and *DestroyRef* are two new RxJS operators introduced in Angular 16 that help manage the lifecycle of a component. These could be used to control when a DOM node should be destroyed and possibly reused. Additionally, the ability to bind router information to component inputs could potentially be used to determine when to reuse a particular DOM node based on the router's state.

However, the specifics of how to implement DOM node re-use in Angular 16 would likely require a deeper dive into these new features and their interaction with Angular's DOM manipulation capabilities. The information provided does not offer a direct example of reusing DOM nodes in Angular 16.

Chapter 4: Speeding Up Your Builds with esbuild in Angular 16

One of the significant enhancements in Angular 16 is the experimental support for the esbuild-based build system. **esbuild** is a relatively new tool in the **JavaScript** ecosystem that aims to provide extremely fast build times for **JavaScript** and **TypeScript** projects. Its speed comes from being written in **Go**, a compiled language, rather than **JavaScript** or **TypeScript**, which are interpreted languages.

Introduction to esbuild

ESBUILD IS AN EXTREMELY fast JavaScript bundler and minifier. It's designed to compile large codebases in a fraction of the time it takes other bundlers. This speed is achieved through a combination of strategies, including parallelism, efficient I/O, inlining, and compiled language performance.

The integration of **esbuild** in Angular 16 has demonstrated a remarkable 72% improvement in cold production builds during the developer preview stage.

Configuring esbuild in Angular 16

IN ANGULAR 16, THE **esbuild** configuration is added to the *"architect"* section of the *angular.json* configuration file. Here is an example:

```
"architect": {
"build": {
"builder": "@angular-devkit/build-angular:browser-esbuild"
}
}
```

In this setup, *@angular-devkit/build-angular:browser-esbuild* is the esbuild builder.

Advantages of Using esbuild in Angular 16

THE PRIMARY ADVANTAGE of using **esbuild** in Angular 16 is the substantial reduction in build times. Faster builds can result in a more responsive and efficient development environment, enabling developers to iterate faster and reducing the wait time between making a change and seeing its effect.

esbuild's speed does not come at the cost of output quality. The resulting JavaScript code is efficient and minified, maintaining the high level of performance that Angular developers have come to expect.

In conclusion, the inclusion of **esbuild** in Angular 16 is a big step forward for build performance, and developers can look forward to significantly improved build times. Although **esbuild** support in Angular 16 is still experimental, the early results are very promising, and developers are encouraged to try it out in their projects.

Chapter 5: Transitioning to Ivy: The Removal of Ngcc

A ngular 16, officially released on May 3, 2023, introduced numerous updates and improvements, with one of the most significant changes being the removal of the *Angular Compatibility Compiler* (*ngcc*). This chapter will explore what *ngcc* is, why it was removed in Angular 16, and what this means for developers.

What is *ngcc*?

THE *Angular Compatibility Compiler* (*ngcc*) was a compiler designed to convert libraries compiled with the **Angular Compiler** (*ngc*) into a format compatible with **Angular Ivy**, the rendering and compiling engine introduced in Angular 9. *ngcc* performed a post-processing transformation of npm packages located in *node_modules*. This transformation ensured **Ivy** compatibility if the library was compiled using the previous **View Engine compiler**.

Why was *ngcc* removed?

THE REMOVAL OF `NGCC` represents the final step in the transition to Ivy, a process that began with the introduction of Ivy in Angular 9. Since then, Angular developers have actively encouraged the community and library authors to switch to Ivy. With the release of Angular 16, this process became final, and now all libraries must be compatible with Ivy.

The removal of `ngcc` simplifies the build process and reduces build time, as there is no longer a need for additional code transformation. It also eases integration with other tools like Webpack and facilitates development and debugging, as there are no complexities associated with having two different library formats.

What does this mean for developers?

FOR MOST DEVELOPERS, the removal of *ngcc* signifies the necessity to ensure that all their dependencies are *Ivy* compatible. If you find that some of your dependencies have not yet been updated, you will have to contact the authors of the library or look for alternatives.

However, the removal of *ngcc* is a significant step forward for Angular, making the framework even more modern and efficient. It means that Angular becomes even faster and lighter, leading to improved performance of your applications.

This change simplifies the development process. Without *ngcc*, applications will compile and run faster, reducing the time spent waiting. In addition, the removal of *ngcc* simplifies the debugging process, as developers will now only have to deal with one library format.

Conclusion

THE REMOVAL OF THE *Angular Compatibility Compiler* (*ngcc*) in Angular 16 is an important step forward in improving the framework's performance and efficiency. This update makes Angular even more modern and faster, leading to improved performance of your applications and facilitating the development process. For developers, this means the necessity to ensure that all their libraries and dependencies are compatible with *Ivy*, but overall, this change brings more benefits than inconveniences.

Chapter 6: Standalone Components: The Power of Independence

Introduction to Standalone Components in Angular 16:

Angular 16 brings forth an exciting new feature called **standalone components**, which revolutionize the way developers build and organize their applications. Standalone components offer a modular approach to Angular development, enabling developers to encapsulate functionality within self-contained entities that can be easily integrated into any Angular project. These components are independent, self-aware entities that enhance code **reusability**, **maintainability**, and **scalability**.

Standalone components in Angular 16 provide several **advantages**. **First** and **foremost**, they promote **modularity** by **encapsulating** the **component's logic**, styles, and HTML templates within a single entity. This encapsulation allows for easy reuse of components across different parts of the application, saving developers valuable time and effort. **Additionally**, **standalone components** adhere to the **principles of separation of concerns**, ensuring that each component is **responsible** for its own **functionality**, resulting in cleaner and more **maintainable codebases**.

The **architecture** of a **standalone component** in Angular 16 consists of three key elements: the **TypeScript** code, the **HTML** template, and the **CSS** styles. The **TypeScript** code defines the component's behavior, including its properties, methods, and lifecycle hooks. The **HTML** template specifies the structure and layout of the component, while the **CSS** styles define its visual appearance.

One of the significant benefits of standalone components is their **flexibility** in **terms of integration**. These components can be seamlessly integrated into existing Angular projects without the need for **NgModule**, eliminating the boilerplate **code associated** with traditional **module-based components**. **Standalone components** can be declared with a standalone attribute, and they cannot be declared within an **NgModule**.

To illustrate the power of standalone components, let's consider an example. Imagine building an e-commerce application where you have a standalone component responsible for displaying product information. This component can be easily reused across various pages, ensuring consistency and reducing redundant code. By encapsulating the component's logic, styles, and HTML templates, you can create a self-contained entity that brings life to the product information and provides a seamless user experience.

In conclusion, standalone components in Angular 16 revolutionize the way developers build applications. With their modular structure, code encapsulation, and reusability, standalone components empower developers to create scalable, maintainable, and efficient Angular projects. Throughout this book, we will explore the intricacies of standalone components, uncovering their architecture, implementation, best practices, and advanced techniques. By the end of this journey, you will have the knowledge and skills to wield the power of standalone components and take your Angular 16 development to new heights.

Architecture of standalone components

THE ARCHITECTURE OF standalone components in Angular 16 provides a modular and self-contained approach to building applications. Standalone components encapsulate their own logic, templates, and styles, offering increased modularity, reusability, and maintainability.

In the context of Angular 16, standalone components are entities that can be easily integrated into any Angular project without the need for NgModule. They follow a modular structure, consisting of three essential elements: the TypeScript code, the HTML template, and the CSS styles.

The TypeScript code defines the behavior and functionality of the standalone component. It includes properties, methods, and lifecycle hooks that allow developers to manipulate and respond to changes in the component's state and environment.

The HTML template specifies the structure and layout of the standalone component. It contains the HTML markup and directives that determine how the component is rendered and interacted with by the user.

The CSS styles define the visual appearance of the standalone component. Styles can be defined inline within the component code or in an external stylesheet. By encapsulating the styles within the component, developers can ensure that the component's visual presentation remains consistent and isolated from other parts of the application.

The architecture of standalone components in Angular 16 promotes the principles of separation of concerns and modularity. Each standalone component is self-contained and independent, allowing for easy reuse and maintenance. Developers can build complex applications by combining and integrating multiple standalone components, leveraging their modular nature to create a cohesive and scalable application architecture.

Furthermore, standalone components offer advantages such as code reusability, isolation for testing, and enhanced scalability. They simplify the development process by reducing the boilerplate code associated with NgModule and promoting a component-centric approach to building applications.

By leveraging the architecture of standalone components in Angular 16, developers can create robust, modular, and maintainable applications. They have the flexibility to customize and fine-tune each component's behavior, appearance, and functionality, resulting in a more engaging and user-friendly application experience.

Here's an example of how you can architect a standalone component in Angular 16

1. CREATE A NEW TYPESCRIPT file for your standalone component, e.g., `my-component.component.ts`:

```typescript
typescript
import { Component } from '@angular/core';
@Component({
selector: 'app-my-component',
template: `
<h1>{{ title }}</h1>
<p>{{ description }}</p>
`,
styleUrls: ['./my-component.component.css']
})
export class MyComponentComponent {
title: string = 'My Standalone Component';
description: string = 'This is a standalone component in Angular 16.';
}
```

2. Create a separate HTML template file, e.g., `**my-component.component.html**`:

```html
html
<h1>{{ title }}</h1>
<p>{{ description }}</p>
```

3. Create a separate CSS file, e.g., `my-component.component.css`:

```css
css
h1 {
color: blue;
}
```

4. In your Angular module or component where you want to use the standalone component, import and declare it:

```typescript
import { MyComponentComponent } from './my-
component.component';
@NgModule({
declarations: [MyComponentComponent],
// ...
})
export class AppModule {}
```

By following this code architecture, you can create a standalone component in Angular 16. The TypeScript file defines the component class with its properties and logic, the HTML template specifies the component's structure, and the CSS file styles the component's elements.

Please note that this is a basic example to illustrate the architecture of a standalone component. In practice, you can extend the component's functionality, add inputs and outputs, utilize Angular services, and apply more advanced techniques as per your project requirements.

Remember to import the necessary dependencies and adjust the file paths according to your project structure.

Implementation of a standalone component

HERE'S AN EXAMPLE OF how you can create a standalone component in Angular 16:

```typescript
import { Component } from '@angular/core';
@Component({
selector: 'app-custom-component',
template: `
<h1>Hello, Standalone Component!</h1>
<p>This is a standalone component in Angular 16.</p>
`,
styles: [
`
h1 {
color: blue;
}
`,
],
})
export class CustomComponent {}
```

In this example, we import the necessary dependencies from Angular core, including the `Component` decorator. We then define our standalone component by using the `@Component` decorator. The `selector` property specifies the HTML tag that will be used to include this component in other templates. The `template` property defines the HTML structure of the component, including the heading and paragraph. The `styles` property allows us to add CSS styles to the component.

By following this example, you can create your own standalone components in Angular 16, encapsulating functionality and enhancing modularity and reusability within your applications.

Best practices of standalone components

WHEN WORKING WITH STANDALONE components in Angular 16, there are several best practices that can help you make the most out of this feature. Here are some key practices to consider:

1. Understand the concept of standalone components

STANDALONE COMPONENTS allow you to declare components, directives, and pipes outside of NgModules, offering flexibility in application structure and reducing the need for NgModule. Familiarize yourself with the concept and benefits of standalone components in Angular 16 [[2](https://blog.ninja-squad.com/2022/05/12/a-guide-to-standalone-components-in-angular/)].

2. Utilize NgRx for state management

CONSIDER USING NGRX, a popular state management system in the Angular ecosystem, for managing application state within standalone components. NgRx follows the Redux implementation of Flux Architecture, providing global-scoped data management [[2](https://blog.bitsrc.io/how-i-have-set-up-ngrx-in-angular-16-with-standalone-components-163499804fbb)].

3. Leverage Declarative Routing

ALTHOUGH ANGULAR LACKS official support for Declarative Routing, you can use packages like Angular Component Router to simplify route configuration within standalone components. Declarative Routing involves declaring routes as elements within component templates, making route configuration more intuitive [[3](https://dev.to/angular/component-first-architecture-with-angular-and-standalone-components-3pjd)].

4. Follow Angular best practices

ADHERE TO GENERAL BEST practices for Angular development to ensure code readability, maintainability, and scalability. Some recommended practices include using Angular CLI for time-saving development tasks, following naming conventions, adhering to component structure guidelines, considering reusability, prioritizing accessibility, optimizing performance, and writing comprehensive tests [[8](https://massivepixel.io/blog/angular-best-practices/)][[10](https://www.telerik.com/blogs/angular-basics-best-practices-creating-new-components)].

5. Consider migration strategies

IF YOU HAVE AN EXISTING Angular solution, you may need to plan for migrating to standalone components. Explore different migration strategies, such as gradually removing Angular modules from the source code while leveraging compatibility between standalone components and modules [[3](https://www.angulararchitects.io/aktuelles/4-ways-to-prepare-for-angulars-upcoming-standalone-components/)][[5](https://stackoverflow.com/questions/74558393/when-to-use-standalone-components-or-modules-in-angular-14)].

6. Test standalone components thoroughly

MAKE SURE TO WRITE comprehensive tests for your standalone components. Angular provides on-board tools like TestBed for setting up tests and supplying components, directives, pipes, and services. Additionally, consider using popular testing frameworks like Cypress and Testing Library to enhance your testing capabilities [[9](https://www.angulararchitects.io/aktuelles/testing-angular-standalone-components/)].

By following these best practices, you can effectively utilize standalone components in Angular 16, ensuring maintainable and scalable code while taking advantage of the flexibility they offer.

Advanced techniques of standalone components

WHEN WORKING WITH STANDALONE components in Angular 16, there are advanced techniques you can employ to enhance your development process and take full advantage of this feature. Here are some advanced techniques to consider:

1. Dynamic Components

LEVERAGE DYNAMIC COMPONENT usage to create components at runtime based on dynamic parameters. Angular provides mechanisms like Dynamic Parameters and the ActivatedRoute class to facilitate dynamic component creation and configuration [[11](https://blog.bitsrc.io/dynamic-components-in-angular-9ddc346e2742)].

2. Component-First State Management

WITH STANDALONE COMPONENTS, NgModules become optional, opening up new possibilities for component-first state management. Explore patterns and techniques for managing state within standalone components, ensuring the development of resilient and scalable applications [[12](https://dev.to/angular/component-first-state-management-for-angular-standalone-components-311a)].

3. Migration Strategies

IF YOU HAVE AN EXISTING Angular solution, consider migration strategies for adopting standalone components. Look for resources and tutorials that specifically cover migrating to standalone components in Angular 15 and 16. These resources can provide insights into the benefits and features of standalone components and guide you through the migration process [[4](https://jasonwatmore.com/angular-15-16-free-course-7-migrate-to-standalone-components-and-functional-interceptors)][[7](https://www.fabiobiondi.dev/tutorials/angular/angular-standalone-apps)].

4. Explore Angular v16 Features

ANGULAR V16 INTRODUCES significant improvements in reactivity, server-side rendering, and tooling. Stay up to date with the latest features and enhancements introduced in Angular v16 to leverage them in your standalone components [[3](https://blog.angular.io/angular-v16-is-here-4d7a28ec680d)].

5. Combine Standalone Components with Other Advanced Angular Techniques

STANDALONE COMPONENTS can be combined with other advanced Angular techniques to further enhance your application development. For example, you can leverage lazy loading, routing, and NgRx state management with standalone components to build more sophisticated and scalable applications [[7](https://www.fabiobiondi.dev/tutorials/angular/angular-standalone-apps)][[9](https://www.angulararchitects.io/aktuelles/testing-angular-standalone-components/)].

6. Follow Angular Best Practices

CONTINUE TO ADHERE to general best practices for Angular development, including code organization, modularity, maintainability, and testing. Following best practices ensures that your standalone components are well-structured, performant, and maintainable [[8](https://massivepixel.io/blog/angular-best-practices/)][[10](https://www.telerik.com/blogs/angular-basics-best-practices-creating-new-components)].

By employing these advanced techniques, you can unlock the full potential of standalone components in Angular 16 and build robust, scalable, and maintainable applications.

Chapter 7: Optimizing JavaScript Bundles with Angular CLI

Configuring Bundling in Angular 16: Best Practices and Techniques

Configuring bundling in Angular 16 is crucial for optimizing the size of the JavaScript bundle and improving the performance of your application. In this post, we will explore best practices and techniques for configuring bundling in Angular 16, enabling you to effectively manage and optimize your application's bundle size.

1. Angular CLI and the angular.json file:

ANGULAR CLI PROVIDES a convenient way to configure bundling in your Angular 16 project. The bundling configuration options are specified in the angular.json file, which is generated for your project. Inside the "projects" section of the angular.json file, you can configure various aspects of bundling, including entry points, output paths, and optimization settings.

2. Code Splitting:

CODE SPLITTING IS A technique that allows you to split your code into smaller, manageable chunks, which are loaded on-demand. By implementing code splitting, you can reduce the initial bundle size and improve the application's loading speed. Angular CLI supports code splitting through lazy loading and dynamic imports. Utilize the Angular Router's lazy loading feature to load modules and components only when required.

3. Optimization and Tree Shaking:

TO OPTIMIZE THE BUNDLE size, Angular CLI performs tree shaking, which eliminates unused code from the final bundle. Make sure to use ES2015 modules (`import` and `export` statements) in your code, as it enables better tree shaking. Additionally, leverage Angular CLI's optimization options, such as minification and dead code elimination, to further reduce the bundle size.

4. Externalizing Dependencies:

IDENTIFY LARGE DEPENDENCIES that are used across multiple modules and consider externalizing them. Externalizing dependencies means loading them separately from your main bundle, which can improve caching and reduce the overall bundle size. Configure the `externals` option in the angular.json file to exclude these dependencies from your bundle and load them externally.

5. Bundle Analysis:

ANALYZING YOUR APPLICATION'S bundle can provide valuable insights into its composition and identify potential areas for optimization. Angular CLI offers built-in tools, like the bundle analyzer, to visualize the size and composition of your bundle. Additionally, there are third-party tools available that provide detailed analysis and recommendations for optimizing your bundle size.

6. Performance Budgets:

SETTING PERFORMANCE budgets is an effective way to control and manage the size of your application's bundle. By defining specific limits for the bundle size, you can ensure that the application remains performant and responsive. **Angular CLI** allows you to configure performance budgets in the **angular.json** file, which generates warnings or errors if the defined thresholds are exceeded.

Conclusion:

CONFIGURING BUNDLING in Angular 16 is essential for optimizing the size of your application's JavaScript bundle and improving performance. By following the best practices and techniques outlined in this post, such as leveraging Angular CLI, implementing code splitting, optimizing with tree shaking, externalizing dependencies, analyzing the bundle, and setting performance budgets, you can effectively manage and optimize your bundle size. By reducing the bundle size, you can enhance the loading speed, improve user experience, and deliver high-performance Angular 16 applications to your users.

Optimizing Bundle Size in Angular 16: Best Practices and Techniques

ANGULAR 16, THE LATEST version of the popular JavaScript framework, introduces several improvements in reactivity, server-side rendering, and tooling. Alongside these enhancements, optimizing bundle size remains a crucial aspect for improving application performance and user experience. These are the best practices and techniques for optimizing bundle size in Angular 16, helping developers deliver faster and more efficient applications.

1. Enable Production Mode

ENABLING PRODUCTION mode is the first step to optimize bundle size. Angular's production mode enables various optimizations like AOT (Ahead-of-Time) compilation and tree shaking, which eliminate unused code and reduce bundle size. Ensure that the

`—prod` flag is used during the build process to enable production mode.

2. Lazy Loading

LAZY LOADING IS A POWERFUL technique to optimize bundle size by loading modules and components only when needed. With lazy loading, you split your application into smaller, feature-based modules and load them on-demand. This approach reduces the initial bundle size and improves application load times. Use the Angular Router's lazy loading feature to implement lazy loading in your application.

3. Code Splitting

CODE SPLITTING IS ANOTHER technique to optimize bundle size by breaking your code into smaller chunks. With code splitting, you can dynamically load specific modules or components when required, reducing the initial payload. Angular CLI provides built-in support for code splitting through the use of dynamic imports and lazy loading.

4. Externalize Dependencies

IDENTIFY AND EXTERNALIZE large dependencies that are commonly used across multiple modules. Angular allows you to exclude these dependencies from your main bundle and load them separately. Utilize techniques like `externals` configuration in Angular CLI's webpack to achieve this. Loading dependencies externally can improve caching and reduce bundle size.

5. Tree Shaking

TREE SHAKING IS A PROCESS that eliminates unused code from your bundles. By leveraging the static structure of your application, the Angular compiler can determine which parts of the code are not used and remove them from the final bundle. Make sure to use ES2015 modules (`import` and `export`) for your code, as it enables better tree shaking.

6. Angular Compiler Options

ANGULAR PROVIDES VARIOUS compiler options that can be configured to optimize bundle size. For example, setting the `fullTemplateTypeCheck` compiler option to `false` can reduce bundle size by disabling template type checking at runtime. Explore the available compiler options and choose the ones that align with your optimization goals.

7. Analyze Bundle Size

TO EFFECTIVELY OPTIMIZE bundle size, it's crucial to analyze the generated bundles. Use tools like Angular CLI's built-in bundle analyzer or third-party tools to analyze the bundle size, identify large dependencies, and optimize accordingly. Understanding the composition of your bundles helps in making informed decisions and applying targeted optimizations.

Conclusion

OPTIMIZING BUNDLE SIZE is essential for improving the performance and loading speed of Angular applications. By following the best practices and techniques mentioned in this article, you can significantly reduce the bundle size of your Angular 16 applications. Enabling production mode, utilizing lazy loading and code splitting, externalizing dependencies, leveraging tree shaking, configuring compiler options, and analyzing bundle size are key steps in achieving optimal bundle size and delivering faster applications to your users.

Remember, optimization is an ongoing process, and it's important to regularly revisit and refine your bundle optimization strategies as your application evolves. With Angular 16's new features and tools, developers have powerful capabilities to optimize bundle size and enhance the overall performance of their Angular applications.

How to implement code splitting, optimizing with tree shaking, externalizing dependencies, analyzing the bundle, and setting performance budgets in Angular 16

TO IMPLEMENT CODE SPLITTING, optimizing with tree shaking, externalizing dependencies, analyzing the bundle, and setting performance budgets in Angular 16, you can follow the instructions below:

1. Code Splitting:

- UTILIZE ANGULAR ROUTER'S lazy loading feature to load modules and components on-demand when they are needed.

- Configure lazy-loaded routes in your Angular application by defining the loadChildren property in your route configuration. The loadChildren property should point to the module file that you want to lazy load.

- Use the **loadChildren** property with the Angular CLI's routing feature to generate separate bundles for each lazy-loaded module.

2. Tree Shaking:

- USE THE ANGULAR CLI'S build optimization features, including the "**build-optimizer**" webpack plugin, which helps remove unused code and reduce the size of the bundle.

- Ensure that your code uses ES2015 modules (`import` and `export` statements) as they enable better tree shaking.

- Avoid importing unnecessary modules or components in your application.

3. Externalizing Dependencies:

- IDENTIFY LARGE DEPENDENCIES that are used across multiple modules and consider externalizing them.

- Configure the `**externals**` option in the angular.json file to exclude these dependencies from your bundle and load them externally.

- Load external dependencies using a CDN or separate script tags in your HTML file.

4. Analyzing the Bundle:

- USE TOOLS LIKE THE source-map-explorer or webpack-bundle-analyzer to analyze the size and composition of your bundle.

- Install the source-map-explorer tool globally using npm or yarn.

- Run the command `**source-map-explorer dist/ my-awesome-project/main.js**` to analyze the bundle size. Ensure that source maps are generated during the build process.

5. Setting Performance Budgets:

- DEFINE PERFORMANCE budgets in the **angular.json** file to control and manage the size of your application's bundle.

- Specify thresholds for bundle size, load time, or other relevant metrics.

- Angular CLI will generate warnings or errors if the defined thresholds are exceeded during the build process.

Please note that these instructions provide a high-level overview of implementing the mentioned techniques. It's recommended to refer to the official Angular documentation and relevant resources for detailed implementation and configuration instructions.

Sources:

- STACK OVERFLOW: [ANGULAR CLI output - how to analyze bundle files](https://stackoverflow.com/questions/46567781/angular-cli-output-how-to-analyze-bundle-files) [[1](https://stackoverflow.com/questions/46567781/angular-cli-output-how-to-analyze-bundle-files)]

- Pluralsight: [Bundling and Code Splitting in Angular](https://www.pluralsight.com/guides/bundling-and-code-splitting-in-angular) [[3](https://www.pluralsight.com/guides/bundling-and-code-splitting-in-angular)]

- Dev.to: [Tree-shakable dependencies in Angular projects](https://dev.to/this-is-angular/tree-shakable-dependencies-in-angular-projects-1ifg) [[4](https://dev.to/this-is-angular/tree-shakable-dependencies-in-angular-projects-1ifg)]

- Telerik: [Speed Up Your Angular Application with Code Splitting](https://www.telerik.com/blogs/speed-up-angular-application-code-splitting) [[5](https://www.telerik.com/blogs/speed-up-angular-application-code-splitting)]

- Stack Overflow: [Angular Tree Shaking: How exactly does it work?](https://stackoverflow.com/questions/60321224/angular-tree-shaking-how-exactly-does-it-work)

[[2](https://stackoverflow.com/questions/60321224/angular-tree-shaking-how-exactly-does-it-work)]

How to improving performance in Angular 16 applications

TO IMPROVE PERFORMANCE in Angular 16 applications, you can follow the following techniques:

1. Rethinking Reactivity:

ANGULAR 16 INTRODUCES a new reactivity model that enhances runtime performance and simplifies the understanding of data flow and view dependencies. Utilize the Angular Signals library, which allows you to define reactive values and express dependencies, reducing computations during change detection and improving overall performance [[1](https://www.itmagination.com/blog/web-dev-angular-16-reactivity-performance-signals)].

2. Identify and Optimize Bottlenecks:

SYSTEMATICALLY IDENTIFY performance bottlenecks in your application. Use tools like Chrome DevTools to analyze performance metrics, identify slow components or functions, and optimize their execution. Optimize heavy computations and reduce unnecessary calculations to improve performance [[2](https://www.simform.com/blog/angular-performance/)].

3. Angular Performance Checklist:

REFER TO COMPREHENSIVE performance checklists to guide your optimization efforts. The Angular Performance Guide provides a checklist with actionable steps to significantly improve the speed of your Angular application [[3](https://danielk.tech/home/complete-angular-performance-guide)].

4. Best Practices:

FOLLOW ANGULAR BEST practices to boost application performance. Implement techniques such as using the trackBy function in ngFor loops to improve rendering performance and lazy loading modules to reduce initial load time. These practices contribute to a smoother user experience and ensure optimal performance [[4](https://akhilabhinav.medium.com/10-angular-best-practices-to-boost-your-application-performance-1a9516c0b09a)].

5. Performance Optimization Techniques:

EXPLORE VARIOUS PERFORMANCE optimization techniques specific to Angular applications. Techniques like code splitting, lazy loading, tree shaking, and differential loading can improve startup time, reduce bundle size, and enhance performance [[5](https://christianlydemann.com/18-performance-optimization-techniques-for-angular-applications-podcast-with-michael-hladky/)].

6. Ahead-of-Time Compilation (AoT):

USE AHEAD-OF-TIME COMPILATION to improve startup times, reduce bundle sizes, and enhance security. AoT compiles the application during the build process, eliminating the need for just-in-time compilation in the browser [[6](https://dev.to/ademking/maximizing-performance-in-angular-applications-proven-tips-and-techniques-41p6)].

7. Bundle Optimization:

OPTIMIZE THE SIZE OF your application bundle by removing unused dependencies, excluding unnecessary polyfills, and utilizing differential loading to serve necessary polyfills based on the user's browser capabilities [[8](https://itnext.io/improve-your-angular-apps-performance-66032f63dc09)].

8. Change Detection Strategy:

CAREFULLY SELECT THE change detection strategy for your components. Consider using the OnPush change detection strategy, which triggers change detection only when input properties change or when an event is fired, reducing unnecessary change detection cycles.

9. Server-side Rendering (SSR):

IMPLEMENT SERVER-SIDE rendering to improve initial page load times and enhance SEO. SSR renders the initial view on the server and sends it to the client, reducing the time to first meaningful paint [[1](https://www.itmagination.com/blog/web-dev-angular-16-reactivity-performance-signals)].

10. Optimize HTTP Requests:

MINIMIZE THE NUMBER of HTTP requests by combining resources, leveraging caching mechanisms, and using efficient data retrieval techniques like pagination or lazy loading for large datasets.

Remember, the performance of an Angular application depends on various factors such as application size, complexity, network conditions, and hardware capabilities. Regular monitoring and profiling using tools like Chrome DevTools can help identify further optimization opportunities.

<u>Sources:</u>

- ANGULAR 16: RETHINKING Reactivity and Improving Performance [[1](https://www.itmagination.com/blog/web-dev-angular-16-reactivity-performance-signals)]

Chapter 8: Simplifying Routing with Component Inputs

I n Angular 16, **simplifying routing** with component inputs can be achieved using the **new feature that allows router data** to be passed **as component inputs**. This feature simplifies the **process of obtaining and using data in components, making** them more **versatile** and **independent** of the **ActivatedRoute** service.

To **bind route parameters to component inputs** in Angular 16, you can follow these steps:

1. Update to Angular 16

MAKE SURE YOU ARE USING Angular version 16 or later to access the new feature.

2. Enable the "bindToComponentInputs" option

IN YOUR APP'S ROUTING configuration, enable the **"bindToComponentInputs"** option when importing the **RouterModule.forRoot**() syntax. This option allows all route data, including static or resolved route data, path parameters, matrix parameters, and query parameters, to be bound to component inputs using the **@Input** decorator [[7](https://www.angulartraining.com/daily-newsletter/angular-16-preview-binding-router-information-to-component-inputs/)].

3. Declare @Input properties in components

IN YOUR COMPONENT, declare the **@Input** properties that will receive the route data. For example, you can use the **@Input** decorator to bind a route parameter to a component input property [[2](https://indepth.dev/posts/1519/router-data-as-components-inputs-in-angular-v16)].

```typescript
import { Component, Input } from '@angular/core';
@Component({
selector: 'app-my-component',
template: '<p>{{ myInput }}</p>',
})
export class MyComponent {
@Input() myInput!: string;
}
```

4. Access the route data in components

ONCE THE @INPUT PROPERTIES are declared, you can directly access the route data within the component. Angular will automatically update the component's property whenever there are changes in the bound route parameter [[2](https://indepth.dev/posts/1519/router-data-as-components-inputs-in-angular-v16)].

```typescript
typescript
import { Component } from '@angular/core';
import { ActivatedRoute } from '@angular/router';
@Component({
selector: 'app-my-component',
template: '<p>{{ myInput }}</p>',
})
export class MyComponent {
constructor(private route: ActivatedRoute) {}
ngOnInit() {
this.myInput = this.route.snapshot.params.myRouteParam;
}
}
```

By binding route data to component inputs, you simplify the process of accessing and utilizing data within components in Angular 16. This new feature improves the developer experience and reduces the manual subscription and retrieval of route parameters [[2](https://indepth.dev/posts/1519/router-data-as-components-inputs-in-angular-v16)].

Chapter 9: Migrating and Scaffolding Standalone Components

———

Migrating to and scaffolding standalone components in Angular 16 offers several benefits, including the elimination of **ngModules** and the ability for components to declare their own dependencies without an ngModule [[5](https://offering.solutions/blog/articles/2023/02/11/migrating-to-angular-standalone-components/)].

To migrate Angular components to new standalone components, you can follow the steps outlined in the Angular documentation. The migration process involves converting components, directives, and pipes to standalone components, removing unnecessary NgModule classes, and bootstrapping the application using standalone APIs [[3](https://timdeschryver.dev/blog/i-tried-the-angular-standalone-migration-and-here-is-the-result)]. Here's a simplified example of how you can migrate a component to a standalone component:

Migrating old Angular component to new Standalone component

1. CREATE A NEW STANDALONE component file (e.g., `my-standalone.component.ts`) and import the necessary dependencies:

typescript
import { Component, Input } from '@angular/core';

2. Decorate the component class with the `@Component` decorator and define the component's selector, template, and styles (if any):

```
typescript
@Component({
selector: 'app-my-standalone',
template: `
<div>
<h1>{{ title }}</h1>
<p>{{ content }}</p>
</div>
`,
styles: [`
div {
background-color: #f0f0f0;
padding: 10px;
}
`]
})
export class MyStandaloneComponent {
@Input() title: string;
@Input() content: string;
}
```

3. Remove the component from any **NgModule** declarations or imports.

4. In the parent component or template where you want to use the standalone component, import the `**MyStandaloneComponent**` and use it like any other component:

```typescript
import { Component } from '@angular/core';
import { MyStandaloneComponent } from './my-standalone.component';
@Component({
selector: 'app-parent',
template: `
<app-my-standalone [title]="myTitle"
[content]="myContent"></app-my-standalone>
`
})
export class ParentComponent {
myTitle = 'Hello';
myContent = 'Welcome to the standalone component!';
}
```

By following these steps, you can migrate your Angular components to new standalone components, simplifying your application structure and eliminating the need for **ngModules**.

Please note that this is a simplified example, and the actual migration process may vary depending on your specific application and the complexity of the components being migrated. It's recommended to refer to the official Angular documentation and resources mentioned above for detailed instructions and best practices.

Scaffolding Standalone Components

TO SCAFFOLD STANDALONE components in Angular 16, you can follow these general steps:

1. Create a new Angular project using the Angular CLI by running the following command:

shell
ng new my-app

2. Change into the project directory:
shell
cd my-app

3. Generate a new standalone component using the Angular CLI:
shell

ng generate component my-standalone

This command will generate a new standalone component named
"***my-standalone***" with its associated files.

4. Use the generated standalone component in your application by
importing it into the desired parent component and adding it to the
template:
typescript
import { Component } from '@angular/core';
import { MyStandaloneComponent } from './my-standalone/my-
standalone.component';
@Component({
selector: 'app-root',
template: `
<h1>Welcome to my app!</h1>
<app-my-standalone></app-my-standalone>
`
})
export class AppComponent {}

Make sure to adjust the paths based on your project's structure.

5. Run the application using the Angular CLI:

shell
ng serve

This command will start a development server, and you can access your application in the browser at `*http://localhost:4200*`.

By following these steps, you can scaffold standalone components in your Angular 16 application. These standalone components can be used independently without the need for *NgModules*. Remember to adjust the names and paths to match your project's structure.

Please keep in mind that the steps outlined above are only a starting point; additional considerations may be necessary depending on the specifics of your project.

Convert an existing Angular project to a standalone project.

ANGULAR 15.2.0 INCLUDES a schematic to assist project authors in converting existing projects to the new standalone APIs. The schematic aims to automatically transform as much code as possible, but some manual fixes by the project author may be required. Execute the following command to run the schematic:

    ng generate @angular/core:standalone

Prerequisites

PLEASE ENSURE THAT the project meets the following requirements before using the schematic:

- Is built with Angular 15.2.0 or later.

- There are no compilation errors.

● Is on a fresh Git branch, and all work has been saved.

Schematic options

OPTION DETAILS

mode	The transformation must be completed. For more information on the available options, see Migration modes below.
path	The migration path in relation to the project root. This option allows you to migrate sections of your project in stages.

Migrations steps

THE MIGRATION PROCEDURE is divided into three steps. You will have to run it several times to ensure that the project builds and behaves as expected.

Run the migration in the following order, ensuring that your code builds and runs between each step:

1. Run ng g @angular/core:standalone and select "Convert all components, directives and pipes to standalone"
2. Run ng g @angular/core:standalone and select "Remove unnecessary NgModule classes"
3. Run ng g @angular/core:standalone and select "Bootstrap the project using standalone APIs"
4. Run any linting and formatting checks, fix any failures, and commit the result

After the migration

CONGRATULATIONS, YOUR application has now been converted to a standalone version. Here are some optional next steps you could take right now:

- Find and remove any remaining NgModule declarations: Because the "Remove unnecessary NgModules" step cannot automatically remove all modules, you may need to manually remove the remaining declarations.

- Run the project's unit tests and correct any errors.

- If the project uses automatic formatting, run any code formatters.

- Run any linters in your project to correct any new warnings. Some linters support a—fix flag that may automatically resolve such warnings.

Migration modes

THE MIGRATION HAS THE following modes:

1. Convert declarations to standalone.
2. Remove unnecessary NgModules.
3. Switch to standalone bootstrapping API. You should run these migrations in the order given.

Convert declarations to standalone

BY SETTING STANDALONE: true and adding dependencies to their imports array, the migration converts all components, directives, and pipes to standalone in this mode.

NgModules that bootstrap a component during this step are ignored by the schematic because they are most likely root modules used by bootstrapModule rather than the standalone-compatible bootstrapApplication. The schematic automatically converts these declarations as part of the "Switch to standalone bootstrapping API" step.

<u>Before:</u>


```typescript
// shared.module.ts
@NgModule({
imports: [CommonModule],
declarations: [GreeterComponent],
exports: [GreeterComponent]
})
export class SharedModule {}
```

```typescript
// greeter.component.ts
@Component({
selector: 'greeter',
template: '<div *ngIf="showGreeting">Hello</div>',
})
export class GreeterComponent {
showGreeting = true;
}
```

After:

```
// shared.module.ts
@NgModule({
imports: [CommonModule, GreeterComponent],
exports: [GreeterComponent]
})
export class SharedModule {}
```

```
// greeter.component.ts
@Component({
selector: 'greeter',
template: '<div *ngIf="showGreeting">Hello</div>',
standalone: true,
imports: [NgIf]
})
export class GreeterComponent {
showGreeting = true;
}
```

Remove unnecessary NgModules

MANY NGMODULES CAN be safely removed after converting all declarations to standalone. This step removes all such module declarations and any corresponding references. If the migration is unable to delete a reference automatically, it leaves the following TODO comment so that the NgModule can be deleted manually:

```
/* TODO(standalone-migration): clean up removed
NgModule¹ reference manually */
```

The migration considers a module to be safe to remove if it:

---

1. https://angular.io/api/core/NgModule

- There are no declarations.

- There are no providers.

- There are no bootstrap components.

- There are no imports that refer to the ModuleWithProviders symbol or a module that cannot be removed.

- There are no classmates. Empty constructors are ignored.

Before:

```
// importer.module.ts
@NgModule({
imports: [FooComponent, BarPipe],
exports: [FooComponent, BarPipe]
})
export class ImporterModule {}
```

After:

```
// IMPORTER.MODULE.TS

// Does not exist!
```

Switch to standalone bootstrapping API

THIS STEP CONVERTS any bootstrapModule usages to the new, standalone bootstrapApplication. It also sets the root component's standalone property to true and deletes the root NgModule. If the root module contains any providers or imports, the migration attempts to copy as much of this configuration into the new bootstrap call as possible.

Before:

```
// ./app/app.module.ts
import { NgModule } from '@angular/core';
import { AppComponent } from './app.component';
@NgModule({
declarations: [AppComponent],
bootstrap: [AppComponent]
})
export class AppModule {}


// ./app/app.component.ts
@Component({ selector: 'app', template: 'hello' })
export class AppComponent {}


// ./main.ts
import { platformBrowser } from '@angular/platform-browser';
import { AppModule } from './app/app.module';
platformBrowser().bootstrapModule(AppModule).catch(e =>
console.error(e));
```

After:

```
// ./app/app.module.ts
// Does not exist!
// ./app/app.component.ts
@Component({ selector: 'app', template: 'hello', standalone: true })
export class AppComponent {}
```

```
// ./main.ts
import { bootstrapApplication } from '@angular/platform-browser';
import { AppComponent } from './app/app.component';
bootstrapApplication(AppComponent).catch(e => console.error(e));
```

Common problems

SOME COMMON ISSUES that may prevent the schematic from working properly are as follows:

- Compilation errors - If the project contains compilation errors, Angular will be unable to properly analyze and migrate it.

- Files not included in a tsconfig - the schematic determines which files to migrate by analyzing the tsconfig.json files in your project. Any files not captured by a tsconfig are not included in the schematic.

- Code that cannot be statically analyzed - the schematic understands your code and determines where to make changes using static analysis. Any classes with metadata that cannot be statically analyzed at build time may be skipped during the migration.

Limitations

BECAUSE OF THE SIZE and complexity of the migration, the schematic cannot handle the following scenarios:

- Because unit tests are not compiled ahead of time (AoT), imports added to components in unit tests may be incorrect.

● The diagram makes use of direct calls to Angular APIs. Custom wrappers around Angular APIs are not recognized by the schematic. For instance, suppose you define a custom customConfigureTestModule function that wraps TestBed there. The components declared by configureTestingModule may not be recognized.

Chapter 10: Required Inputs: Enforcing Component Directives

⸻

Enforcing Component Directives in Angular 16 allows you to specify how components should be instantiated, processed, and used at runtime. Component directives, along with structural and attribute directives, are the three types of directives in Angular.

To create a custom directive in Angular, you can use the Angular command-line tool. The specific command to create a custom directive is not provided in the available information. However, the general syntax to create a custom directive is as follows:

shell

ng generate directive directiveName

This command generates a new directive with the specified `directiveName`. Once the directive is created, you can use it in your component by adding it to the `directives` array in the component's metadata.

For example, suppose you have a custom directive called `MyDirective`. To use it in a component, you would import the directive and add it to the `directives` array:

```typescript
import { MyDirective } from './my.directive';
@Component({
// Component metadata
...
directives: [MyDirective]
})
export class MyComponent {
// Component logic
}
```

By enforcing the component directive in this way, the Angular framework ensures that the specified directive is used within the component.

It's important to note that the specific implementation and usage of component directives may vary based on your specific requirements and application structure.

Chapter 11: Understanding takeUntilDestroyed and DestroyRef

In Angular 16, there are features like `takeUntilDestroyed` and `DestroyRef` that help simplify the process of unsubscribing from observables in Angular components, preventing memory leaks.

The `takeUntilDestroyed` feature is a new approach introduced in Angular 16 that automates the unsubscription process when subscribing to observables. It simplifies the code and improves readability by automatically handling unsubscription based on the component's lifecycle. By using the `takeUntil` operator along with a `Subject`, the `takeUntilDestroyed` feature ensures that the subscriptions are properly unsubscribed when the component is destroyed.

On the other hand, `DestroyRef` is another feature introduced in Angular 16. It allows you to create a reusable function for cleanup logic, ensuring that resources associated with a component are properly released. This feature can be helpful for managing cleanup tasks, such as unsubscribing from observables, removing event listeners, or performing any necessary cleanup operations.

These features provide a convenient way to handle subscription cleanup and prevent memory leaks in Angular applications.

Please note that the specific implementation and usage of these features may vary based on your application's requirements and coding style.

Sample code to Understanding takeUntilDestroyed and DestroyRef

HERE'S AN EXAMPLE OF code that demonstrates the usage of `takeUntilDestroyed` and `DestroyRef` in Angular 16:

```typescript
import { Component, OnDestroy } from '@angular/core';
import { takeUntilDestroyed, DestroyRef } from 'angular-destroy-ref';
@Component({
selector: 'app-example',
template: '<p>Example Component</p>',
})
export class ExampleComponent implements OnDestroy {
destroyRef = new DestroyRef();
ngOnInit(): void {
// Subscribe to an observable and use takeUntilDestroyed
someObservable
.pipe(takeUntilDestroyed(this.destroyRef))
.subscribe((data) => {
// Handle the data
});
}
ngOnDestroy(): void {
// Call the destroy method to clean up subscriptions
this.destroyRef.destroy();
}
}
```

In this example, we import the `DestroyRef` class from the `angular-destroy-ref` package. We create an instance of `DestroyRef` called `destroyRef` in the component. Inside the `ngOnInit` method, we subscribe to an observable and use the `takeUntilDestroyed` operator with `destroyRef` to automatically unsubscribe from the observable when the component is destroyed. This ensures that there are no memory leaks.

In the `ngOnDestroy` method, we call the `destroy` method of `destroyRef` to clean up any remaining subscriptions.

Please note that `takeUntilDestroyed` and `DestroyRef` are not built-in Angular features but rather examples of community libraries or concepts. You may need to install the `angular-destroy-ref` package or adapt the code to match the specific library or implementation you are using.

Chapter 12: Styling Your Angular Applications with Tailwind CSS

Styling plays a crucial role in creating visually appealing and user-friendly web applications. In Angular 16, developers have the flexibility to choose from various CSS frameworks to enhance their styling workflow. One popular choice is Tailwind CSS, a utility-first CSS framework known for its simplicity and flexibility. In this, we will explore how to integrate Tailwind CSS into an Angular 16 project and leverage its utility classes to style our Angular applications.

Prerequisites

BEFORE WE BEGIN, ENSURE that you have the following set up:

- Angular CLI installed on your machine

- An Angular 16 project created using the Angular CLI

Step 1: Install Tailwind CSS

To integrate Tailwind CSS into our Angular project, we need to install the necessary dependencies. Open a terminal or command prompt and navigate to your project directory. Run the following command to install Tailwind CSS via npm:

npm install tailwindcss

Step 2: Configure Tailwind CSS

After installing Tailwind CSS, we need to generate a configuration file to customize its settings. In the terminal, run the following command to generate a `tailwind.config.js` file:

npx tailwindcss init

This command generates a default configuration file that you can modify according to your project requirements. Open the `tailwind.config.js` file and customize the template paths to match your Angular project's structure.

Step 3: Add Tailwind Directives to styles.css

Next, we need to import the Tailwind CSS styles into our project's main styles file (`**styles.css**` by default). Open the `**styles.css**` file and add the following `**@import**` statements at the top:

```css
@import 'tailwindcss/base';
@import 'tailwindcss/components';
@import 'tailwindcss/utilities';
```

THESE IMPORTS WILL bring in the base styles, component styles, and utility classes provided by Tailwind CSS.

Step 4: Start the Angular Development Server

With Tailwind CSS set up in our Angular project, we can now start the development server to see the styles in action. In the terminal, run the following command:

```
ng serve
```

This command will build the Angular project and start the development server. Open your web browser and navigate to `**http://localhost:4200**` to view your Angular application with Tailwind CSS styles applied.

Step 5: Using Tailwind Utility Classes

Tailwind CSS provides a wide range of utility classes that allow us to style elements by applying pre-defined classes directly in our HTML markup. For example, to apply a margin to an element, we can use the `m-{size}` class, where `{size}` can be `1`, `2`, `3`, and so on. Similarly, there are utility classes for colors, typography, spacing, and more.

Integrating Tailwind CSS into your Angular 16 project can greatly enhance your styling workflow. By following the steps outlined in this article, you can easily set up Tailwind CSS, configure it according to your project's needs, and start leveraging its utility classes to style your Angular applications. With its simplicity and flexibility, Tailwind CSS provides a powerful toolset for creating visually stunning and responsive web applications.

Remember to experiment with the utility classes provided by Tailwind CSS and explore its extensive documentation to discover more styling options and techniques.

How to use Tailwind CSS in Standalone Components

TO USE TAILWIND CSS in standalone components in Angular 16, you can follow these steps:

1. Create an Angular Project:

If you haven't already, start by creating a new Angular project using Angular CLI. Run the command `ng new project-name` to generate a new Angular project.

2. Install Tailwind CSS:

Next, install Tailwind CSS in your Angular project. You can use npm to install Tailwind CSS by running the command `npm install tailwindcss`.

3. Configure Tailwind CSS:

After installing Tailwind CSS, you need to configure it for your project. Generate a Tailwind configuration file by running the command `npx tailwindcss init`. This will create a `tailwind.config.js` file in your project's root directory.

4. Include Tailwind CSS in Angular Styles:

In the `styles.scss` file of your Angular project (located in the `src` folder), import the Tailwind CSS styles by adding the following line at the beginning of the file:

```scss
@import 'tailwindcss/base';
@import 'tailwindcss/components';
@import 'tailwindcss/utilities';
```

This imports the base, components, and utilities styles provided by Tailwind CSS.

5. Use Tailwind CSS Classes in Standalone Components:

With Tailwind CSS configured, you can now use its utility classes in your standalone Angular components. Apply the desired classes directly to HTML elements in your component's template to style them accordingly. For example:

```html
<div class="bg-blue-500 text-white p-4">This is a Tailwind CSS component.</div>
```

In the above example, the `**bg-blue-500**`, `**text-white**`, and `**p-4**` classes from Tailwind CSS are applied to a `div` element, setting its background color to blue, text color to white, and adding padding.

6. Build and Run Your Angular Project:

Once you've added Tailwind CSS classes to your standalone components, you can build and run your Angular project using the Angular CLI. Run the command `ng serve` to start the development server and view your application in the browser.

By following these steps, you can use Tailwind CSS in standalone components within your Angular 16 project. Tailwind CSS provides a wide range of utility classes to style your components efficiently and consistently.

Chapter 13: Advanced Angular 16 Techniques

When it comes to advanced techniques in Angular 16, there are several resources available that can help you enhance your skills and build more sophisticated web applications. Here are some references to explore:

1. Angular: Advanced Tips and Best Practices for Experts and Beginners: This article provides best practices, pitfalls, and recommendations for building Angular applications. It covers topics such as following Angular's recommendations and style guide, using UI component libraries like Angular Material or primeng, and staying up to date with the latest Angular versions. [[1](https://dzone.com/articles/angular-advance-tips-amp-best-practices-for-expert)]

2. Angular Core Deep Dive - Beginner to Advanced (Angular 16): This Udemy course offers a comprehensive guide to the advanced features of Angular. It covers topics like change detection, style isolation, dependency injection, content projection, internationalization, and standalone components. The course is designed for beginners and progresses to intermediate and advanced topics. [[2](https://www.udemy.com/course/angular-course/)]

3. 5 tips to boost your Angular skills: This article shares five tips to enhance your Angular skills, including understanding change detection, using the OnPush mode, leveraging @HostListener for event subscriptions, using the async pipe with RxJS streams, and following Angular's coding patterns. [[3](https://indepth.dev/posts/1307/5-tips-to-boost-your-angular-skills)]

4. "Mastering Angular 16: Advanced Techniques for Web Development": This book provides comprehensive coverage of advanced Angular techniques. It covers fundamental concepts like components, modules, templates, and data binding, as well as more advanced topics like routing, state management with RxJS, HTTP communication, error handling, forms and validation, and Angular Material components. It offers hands-on examples and step-by-step instructions. [[4](Mastering-Angular-16-Techniques-Development-ebook/dp/B0C622MDHJ)]

5. Advanced Angular Online Training Course: This online training course offers in-depth coverage of advanced Angular concepts, RxJS, and NgRx. It focuses on hands-on learning through workshops and real-time app building. The course is designed for individuals with significant experience in Angular and TypeScript. [[6](https://www.angularacademy.ca/courses/advanced-angular-training)]

6. 10 Advanced Angular Techniques to Level Up Your Development Skills: This article presents ten advanced techniques to improve your Angular development skills. It covers topics such as OnPush change detection, dynamic component loading, lazy loading modules, optimizing HTTP requests, using reactive forms, and leveraging Angular's animation capabilities. [[7](https://blog.josematos.work/10-advanced-angular-techniques-to-level-up-your-development-skills-5026626bbaa1)]

7. ANGULAR: Advanced level (2023 Edition): This Udemy course aims to teach you how to build professional web applications using Angular. It covers both the basics and advanced features of Angular and provides hands-on guidance. The course is suitable for beginners and does not require prior Angular experience. [[8](https://www.udemy.com/course/angular-professional-level/)]

MASTERING ANGULAR 16: A CONCISE OVERVIEW

Remember to explore these resources to deepen your knowledge of Angular 16 and take your development skills to the next level.

Chapter 14: Best Practices for Angular 16 Development

Use Angular CLI

Angular comes with its own command line. It's highly recommended to install it and use it as much as possible. Using predefined commands instead of doing everything by hand is incredibly time-saving. For example, making a new Angular project manually would probably take an hour or two (don't try that unless you're an absolute masochist). But it can be easily done with just one command:

ng new nameOfTheApplication

After that, you can immediately run the application:

ng serve

Using the Command–line Interface tool, you can generate any type of file available for Angular — be it a component, interface, service, or anything else. Also, you can search through official documentation using the CLI. The following command:

ng doc <search keyword>

should prompt the opening of a browser with search results for a given keyword on the Angular official page.

The main benefits of using CLI are:

- Saved time,

- Platform independence,

● Effortless configuration while adding new code.

Follow the file naming convention

THERE'S A CLEAR AND logical file naming convention defined by the authors of the Angular framework. It goes:
[name].[role].[extension]

If there is more than one word, you can use kebab-case:
[name].[role-with-a-kebab-case].[extension].

That's why the default module after you created a new Angular app with CLI, called **AppModule**, is composed of the following files:
app.component.html
app.component.scss
app.component.spec.ts
app.component.ts
app.module.ts.

If you use the CLI to create new files for you, then you will be following the convention automatically. If there's an extraordinary situation and you need to create files by yourself, then stick to this convention to make life easier for other developers — they will recognize this naming schema at a first glance and have no trouble figuring out what's going on in the code.

The main benefits of following this convention are:

● Easy recognition of what the file does,

● Searching and grouping concrete files is easy.

Have a clear folder structure

NOT ONLY THERE'S A file naming convention, but also a recommendation for the folder structure. And It's just as important.

You can see the proper structure below:

That's how it may look like after creating some components. The directories are created automatically by the CLI. You can create some extra folders to group it even more, just remember to use clear names.

Below, you can see a more complicated structure for a store where all elements are grouped in the directories by their roles.

The main benefits of having a clear folder structure are:

- Easy recognition of where the files responsible for specific features are,

- Higher visibility of code dependencies,

- Searching and grouping concrete files is easy.

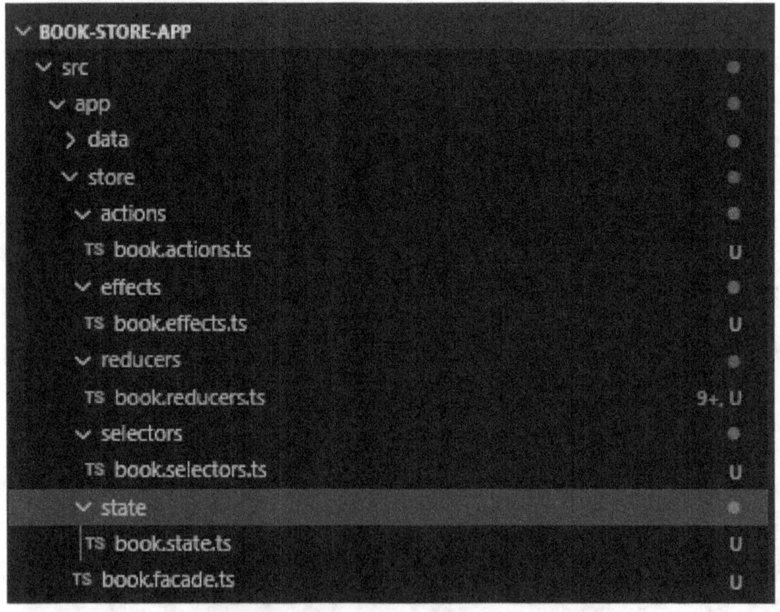

Rule of one (one file per object)

It's a simple rule mentioned on the official Angular page. It says you should have only one object per file. So, for example, don't put an interface on top of your class. Create a new file to have it there.

It also helps to comply with the single responsibility principle.

The main benefit of having one object per file is a clear indication of what's inside. This can be a life–saver when working on big projects.

Distinguish variable and class names, dumb and smart components

Let's look into the files and take something simple — classes, for instance.

The name of the class should follow **PascalCase** naming convention, for example: **AppComponent**. The name of class properties and methods should use **camelCase**, resulting in **appName**.

The very basic structure in Angular is a component. It's popular and useful to divide your components into dumb (presentational) and smart (logical) components. The dumb components are responsible for presenting data and they rarely have any logic on their own (if they do, it's probably related to the UI, not application state), while the smart components take care of performing functions and managing data — sending the relevant data to dump components included.

The benefits of having proper variable and class names and dumb and smart components are:

- Easy recognition of classes and variables by name only,

- Easy recollection of where to change the UI and where to change the logic,

- Easier creation of reusable components.

Use ESLint

ANGULAR DOESN'T COME with the linter (the plugin that ensures the following of certain code writing rules) but you can easily fix that by running this line:

```
ng add @angular-eslint/schematics
```

Then, some modern code editor like Visual Studio Code will automatically lint it for you. Otherwise, you can lint your code with a simple command:

```
ng lint
```

After that, you're all set to lint your code. It has some good predefined settings but you can configure them however you wish — for example, to set some additional warnings or errors. All the configuration is stored in the .eslintrc.json file.

You can check out the complete list of rules to see what's included in the recommended settings and what isn't. Additionally, you can read in−depth explanations for each rule.

The main benefits of using the ESLints are:

- The same code convention is followed throughout the whole Angular application,

- Rules verification in an automated way during the build process,

- Easy updates and additions of new rules to the coding style guide.

- Use TypeScript strict mode

Since the version 12 and up, each new project created with the CLI has a TypeScript strict mode enabled by default, so you might not even realize that you're using it. The strict mode is a set of rules that enforce specific methods of writing code. It contains noImplicitAny, noImplicitThis, strictBindCallApply, strictNullChecks, strictFunctionTypes, strictPropertyInitialization and alwaysStrict.

Many of them are self-explanatory and you can turn them on/off in the tsconfig.json file. You can do the same to the whole strict mode by changing this property:

"strict": true

The main benefit of using TypeScript strict mode is a better–crafted code because of enforced rules.

Break down and reuse your components

DURING ANGULAR DEVELOPMENT, it's easy to create big components with similar logic repeated many times throughout the application. But it's a much better option to create small, reusable components. You also should keep in mind their dumb and smart versions.

The main benefits of breaking down and reusing your components are:

- Easy maintenance because of small components,

- Saved time because of the reusable components.

Use interfaces

IT'S VERY LIKELY YOU will operate on some data from the API. It usually has a predefined JSON format. It's extremely good to have it typed with interfaces instead of using any. The interfaces in Angular allow specifying whether the property is mandatory (by default) or optional (you need to add ? after the property name).

Here's a simple example:

```
export interface BookState {
books: Book[];
loaded: boolean;
error?: string | null;
}
```

THE MAIN BENEFITS OF using interfaces are:

- Fewer bugs,

- Predictable data that's easy to operate on.

Use safe navigation operator (also known as optional chaining)

WHO HAS NEVER SEEN the error 'cannot read property of undefined'?

Nobody?

Yeah, that's what I thought.

In many cases, this error is a result of not using a safe navigation operator. It's a critical error, so when it happens, Angular will not render the component. It can be prevented with a simple construction like this:

```
objectMayBeUndefined.property
```

It's equivalent to writing an if, like this:

```
if(objectMayBeUndefined)
objectMayBeUndefined.property
```

In this case, the question mark is called a safe navigation operator.

The main benefits of using a safe navigation operator are:

No critical errors when the property is not present,

Reduced number of ifs in the code,

Easy prediction of what might not be present at the time of execution.

Create index.ts files

If you're developing a big application, you'll probably end up exporting and importing a lot of elements into the app. When there's a lot to export, it's best to use a single file to accumulate all exports.

The simple index.ts would look like this:
export * from './hero.model.ts';
export * from './hero.service.ts';
export { AppComponent } from './app.component.ts';

You can export the object from the file or use barrel exports.

The main benefit of using an index.ts file is having one-source of truth for what's being exported.

Rely on OnPush change detection strategy

IN ORDER TO REFLECT changes to the state of the application each frontend framework needs some kind of change detection mechanism, and to do it in a performant way that won't kill the browser, each framework needs to be optimised so that re-renders don't occur unnecessarily. Angular is no different.

By default, it will react to all of the actions that happen both synchronously and asynchronously. Each change to your @Input (even properties nested somewhere deep inside the object), each event, browser API call (like setTimeout, scroll event etc.), will trigger change detection. It happens because Angular does not know all possible ways that your data can change. It needs to "just work", so it reacts to everything.

To optimize that, you can opt-in to use OnPush change detection strategy that will greatly reduce the number of re-renders, but can also cause your view to not reflect your current state correctly. When you use OnPush, only changes to your @Inputs (in case of objects, reference to new object must be passed) and Observable emits that are caught by the async pipe trigger change detection. If you need to re-render in other situations, you have to tell Angular to do it by using either markForCheck or detectChanges methods from ChangeDetectorRef.

To start relying on OnPush, a developer has to explicitly indicate when Angular should detect new changes. You can do this by adding a simple line to the component declaration:

```
@Component({
selector: 'app-root',
templateUrl: './app.component.html',
styleUrls: ['./app.component.scss'],
changeDetection: ChangeDetectionStrategy.OnPush
})
export class AppComponent {
...
}
```

The main benefits of relying on onPush are:

- Increased performance,

- More control over the change detection process.

Don't use type any

ANGULAR ALLOWS YOU to use a general type any that's used to match anything. It's easy to spot — it might result in many errors like property name typos, type mismatch, potential undefined value, etc. For example:

```
metaData: any;
<div class="card-container">
<button (click)="addBook()">{{ metaData.numberOfBoks+1 }}
books already there</button>
</div>
```

Using type any can be especially disastrous for complicated objects that should've had their own interface. Also, any doesn't allow IDE to recognize what's inside the variable so it can't help you with useful autocorrect or error highlighting. The easiest way to ensure that any wouldn't be used is to configure ESLint to take care of it. Otherwise, you can just check manually if it's not in the code.

The main benefits of not using type any are:

- More self–explanatory code,

- Fewer bugs,

- Easier debugging in case of errors.

Don't use the scroll event

EVENTS ARE ACTIONS that happen due to user activity on the website — like a clicked button, refreshed page, or an opened new window. You can define your own events but many of them are predefined. You can listen to all possible events to execute a function when triggered.

One of such events is a scroll event. It's triggered when a user scrolls a website. It means you can easily generate millions of function executions while listening to this event. There are ways to mitigate it like debounce but it's best to try to avoid it as much as possible.

The main benefit of not using the scroll event is an increase in performance.

Use Built-In Angular Features For DOM Operations

FROM TIME TO TIME, you've got to manipulate DOM elements in HTML. Because Angular is based on TypeScript, which is a tyYou might find yourself in a situation where you need direct access to DOM elements. Technically, using APIs built directly into the browser will work, but in most cases that is not what you should use.

Fortunately, authors of the framework created their own way to deal with it. The simplest way to use it is to tag the element in the template:
<result-score #winnerResult [result]="result"></result-score>

Then, you can refer to this element in the script file:
@ViewChild("winnerResult") winnerResult: WinnerResultComponent;

This method allows you to operate from the parent perspective on the child component (in this case, WinnerResultComponent). You'll most likely want to operate not only on your components but on native elements as well. If you tagged regular HTML element, ViewChild decorator would return ElementRef. To query elements that were projected using, you can use ContentChild decorator instead.

To manipulate or create new elements in the DOM, `Renderer2` should be used unless you know what you are doing. Manipulating elements directly might get your data model and the view out of sync, since it does not trigger change detection. Also, DOM manipulation works only in the browser, so when you use Angular Universal you might encounter problems.

The main benefits of using Angular features for DOM manipulation are:

- Performance increase,

- Easy code maintenance,

Don't use functions and impure pipes in your HTML template

ANGULAR OFFERS A DIRECT connection between HTML templates and script files. It's also possible to use functions and pipes. Here's an example of such a code:

```
<div class="card-container">
<strong> {{ title | transform }}: <input type="text" name="title" #title /></strong>
<strong> {{ author | transform }}: <input type="text" name="author" #author /></strong>
<strong> {{ year | transform }}: <input type="number" name="year" #year /></strong>
</div>
<div class="card-container">
<button (click)="addBook()">{{ textButton() }}</button>
</div>
```

The problem with the functions and impure pipes is connected to the change detection mechanism. When Angular does the change detection, it doesn't know what exactly has changed so all functions and impure pipes are recalculated — textButton() and | transform in the code above. If there are a lot of them in the template, it might impact the whole Angular application significantly.

The main benefits of not using functions and impure pipes in HTML template are:

- Huge performance increase,

- Better code organization.

Use trackBy in ngFor

NGFOR IS A STANDARD construction to do loops in the HTML templates. It's a very comfortable way to operate on the recurring code on many data instances. It works without any issues if your data is static. Otherwise, all elements are updated once data changes, even those that stayed the same. So let's check this example:

```
public array: Result[] = [
{ id: 1, result: 123412423 },
{ id: 2, result: 234912423 },
{ id: 3, result: 341242983 }
];
public getIdTracking(index: int, item: Result) {
return item.id;
}
```

Now, let's add a new element to the array with two implementations of ngFor:

```
<div *ngFor="let i of array">
...
</div>
```

Here, 4 elements will be evaluated.

```
<div *ngFor="let i of array; trackBy: getIdTracking">
...
</div>
```

Here, there'll be only one element evaluated.

The main benefit of using trackBy in ngFor is increased performance.

Take care of performance with Angular Differs API

ANGULAR DIFFERS API isn't as popular as it should be. The main idea is to have a clear picture of what has been changed, instead of just the information that the change was made.

Angular Differs API contains two Differs API options:

1. IterableDiffer, which tracks changes made to the iterable over time and exposes methods to react to these changes,
2. KeyValueDiffers, which tracks changes made to the object over time and exposes methods to react to these changes.

The main benefit of using Angular Differs API is increased performance.

Take advantage of the state management for API calls

DOES YOUR APP CALL the API? Are you dealing with asynchronous calls?

I guess the answers are yes and yes.

Then, you definitely need state management. State management is a way to deal with asynchronous actions and keep fetched data in an organized way. There are many ways to do that — for example, by using NgRx.

The main benefits of using the state management are:

- Easy to debug data flow in Angular applications,

- Split between the management of API calls and other code.

Use lazy loading

USUALLY, BIG APPLICATIONS contain a lot of routes. It's a good practice to use lazy loading to load the module for a route that's actually needed, not for all of them. It's just one line in the code called loadChildren:

```
...
{
path: 'adminDashboard',
loadChildren: () =>
import('./admin-dashbaord/admin-dashbaord.module').then(
(m) => m.AdminDashbaordModule
),
}
...
```

If you'd like to learn more about it, go to this article.

The main benefit of using lazy load is increased performance.

Use SCAM module schema

THERE'S A RELATIVELY new idea to organize your module in the SCAM (Single Component Angular Modules) schema. In short, it promotes creating a module for each component. This helps to avoid all the issues that come up while using NgModules — for example, troublesome refactoring.

SCAM will become especially important with the incoming implementation of the standalone components, which has a great chance of becoming the hottest topic in Angular next year. You can check out the whole discussion in the official Angular repository.

The main benefits of using SCAM module schema are:

- Easy-to-follow structure of the project,

- Being ready to transfer components into standalone ones when they're implemented.

Write comments only when it makes sense

PUTTING COMMENTS INTO the code is a good practice, but only when they convey a useful message to the reader later on. The comments describing what the code does aren't good comments. Well–written code should explain itself, without the need for additional descriptions.

Good comments either should describe how and when to use a part of the code (many libraries have docs comments for their functions, including parameters) or describe unusual structures, like atypical bug fixes for older browsers.

The main benefits of writing comments only when it makes sense are:

- Easier to understand code,

Write tests

WRITING TESTS MAY SEEM like an unnecessary overhead but it's a vital practice for all developers. Local unit tests and final automated end-to-end tests are valuable assets to detect bugs early. Writing tests may take some of your time at first, but it will pay off in the future — for example, when you'll have to compare old and new functionalities after applying changes.

The main benefits of writing tests are:

- Faster development process,

- Reduced number of bugs,

- Enabled Test–Driven Development.

Don't forget about DRY, KISS, SOLID, YAGNI, BDUF, SOC, and other wise acronyms.

Since programming became really popular, the creation of code writing principles was inevitable. These principles are general enough to be applied to all programming languages, so Angular, which is written in TypeScript, can also make use of them.

Because all the principles are rather long, developers created acronyms for them. The most popular ones are:

- DRY (Don't Repeat Yourself)

- KISS (Keep It Stupid Simple)

- SOLID

- S — Single–Responsibility Principle

- O — Open–Closed Principle

- L — Liskov Substitution Principle

- I — Interface Segregation Principle

- D — Dependency Inversion Principle

- YAGNI (You Aren't Gonna Need It)

- BDUF (Big Design Up Front)

- SOC (Separation Of Concerns)

Summary: Angular best practices

ALL THESE BEST PRACTICES described didn't show up out of anywhere — they're the result of the long and hard work of Angular developers. They've been proven many times before and are extensively battle-tested.

When it comes to best practices for Angular 16 development, there are several resources available that provide valuable insights and recommendations. Here are some references to explore:

1. 24 Angular Best Practices You Shouldn't Code Without: This article emphasizes the importance of Angular best practices for unlocking the full potential of the framework. It covers practices such as using Angular CLI for efficient project setup and management, generating different types of Angular files, and accessing official documentation. [[1](https://massivepixel.io/blog/angular-best-practices/)]

2. Angular: Advanced Tips and Best Practices for Experts and Beginners: This article provides best practices, pitfalls, and recommendations for building Angular applications. It suggests following Angular's recommendations, reading the Angular style guide, and utilizing resources like the "Tour of Heroes" tutorial and the Angular Glossary. It also mentions the importance of staying updated

with Angular versions using update.angular.io. [[5](https://dzone.com/articles/angular-advance-tips-amp-best-practices-for-expert)]

3. Angular modules: Best practices for structuring your app: This tutorial focuses on structuring an Angular application using modules for improved reusability and maintainability. It explains the concept of Angular modules, their benefits, and provides a practical example of building an ecommerce app. [[6](https://blog.logrocket.com/angular-modules-best-practices-for-structuring-your-app/)]

4. Angular Best Practices in 2023 To Build Web Applications: This article highlights Angular best practices, including the use of Angular CLI for initializing, developing, maintaining, testing, and debugging Angular applications. It emphasizes the importance of leveraging Angular's core components, such as modules, components, metadata, templates, data binding, services, directives, and dependency injection. [[8](https://www.albiorixtech.com/blog/angular-best-practices/)]

5. Angular Basics: Best Practices for Creating a New Angular Project: This guide provides best practices for creating successful Angular projects, catering to both beginners and experienced developers. It emphasizes the importance of optimizing performance, enhancing user experience, SEO, cost reduction, scalability, and maintainability. [[9](https://www.telerik.com/blogs/angular-basics-best-practices-creating-new-project)]

6. Adopting the Best Practices in Angular Development in 2023: This blog aims to provide a list of best practices for Angular developers, including keeping components small and focused, utilizing reactive programming techniques with RxJS, following proper error handling and logging, utilizing Angular CLI, applying modular architecture, and optimizing performance. These practices enhance reusability, testability, efficiency, and separation of concerns in Angular

applications. [[10](https://levelup.gitconnected.com/adopting-the-best-practices-in-angular-development-77b572a680d3)]

7. Angular Best Practices for 2021: This article highlights best practices for Angular development, starting with the use of Angular CLI. It emphasizes practices such as following modular architecture, leveraging TypeScript for static typing, utilizing Angular's features for building enterprise applications, and using community projects like Ionic, NativeScript, and Electron for creating native apps. [[11](https://dev.to/grapecity/angular-best-practices-for-2021-e7)]

Remember to explore these resources to gain a deeper understanding of best practices for Angular 16 development and apply them to your projects for improved code quality, maintainability, and scalability.

Chapter 15: Building a Real-World Project with Angular 16 a Bookstore

To find more details and finish this project, visit the GitHub page at https://github.com/icpmtech/book-mastering-angular-16[1]. Use an editor to make changes and follow the given instructions. For any inquiries or issues, go to Cantinhode.net. All steps are documented on GitHub.

---

1. https://github.com/icpmtech/book-mastering-angular-16

PEDRO MARTINS

About Author

Pedro Martins
Software/Solution Architect

Extensive experience in analyzing, designing, implementing, and managing systems. Participated in a variety of commercial and industry projects, including healthcare consulting, construction industry solutions, financial institutions, banking, ticketing, interactive television, competitiveness analysis, business analysis, and others. I created a website (https://cantinhode.net) to help the coding community grow and to share insights into my work. The website includes opinion articles, practical examples, and my resume, all with the goal of encouraging the development of technical solutions for information systems architecture across various domains, programming languages, and on-premises and cloud solutions.

Don't miss out!

Visit the website below and you can sign up to receive emails whenever Pedro Martins publishes a new book. There's no charge and no obligation.

https://books2read.com/r/B-A-ARGZ-EDFLC

BOOKS 2 READ

Connecting independent readers to independent writers.

About the Author

Have an extensive experience in analyzing, designing, implementing, and managing systems. Participated in a variety of commercial and industry projects, including healthcare consulting, construction industry solutions, financial institutions, banking, ticketing, interactive television, competitiveness analysis, business analysis, and others. Creator of the website https://cantinhode.net to help the coding community grow and to share insights about coding. The website includes opinion articles, practical examples, all with the goal of encouraging the development of technical solutions for information systems architecture across various domains, programming languages and on-premises and cloud solutions.

Read more at https://cantinhode.net.